# The Italians on Delos

Claire HASENOHR

ÉCOLE FRANÇAISE D'ATHÈNES
ΓΑΛΛΙΚΗ ΣΧΟΛΗ ΑΘΗΝΩΝ

# Preliminary note

The numbers ringed in red ① refer to the cover flap maps.

The proposed itinerary (p. 29 onwards) is marked by a red dashed line on the back flap.

Abbreviations: *ID* = P. Roussel, M. Launay, *Inscriptions de Délos* (1937); *SEG* = *Supplementum Epigraphicum Graecum*; *EAD* = *Exploration archéologique de Délos*; *BCH* = *Bulletin de correspondance hellénique*.

# Chronology

**314–167**: Delos is an independent city, home to an international sanctuary of Apollo and a regional port of commerce.

**172–168**: the Third Macedonian War: Roman victory over Perseus, king of Macedon.

**167**: the Roman Senate hands Delos over to Athens, which expels the Delians from the island and establishes a cleruchy there.

**before 149/8**: founding of the association of the Poseidoniasts of Berytos on Delos.

**146**: Rome's victory over the Achaean League and destruction of Corinth.

**133**: Attalus III bequeaths the kingdom of Pergamon to Rome.

**129**: the kingdom of Pergamon becomes the Roman province of Asia.

**c.130–120**: large numbers of Italians move to Delos. Founding of the association of the *Italici*?

**before 125**: building works of the *epimeletes* of the island Theophrastos around the port of Delos and in the agora that bears his name.

**90–88**: the Social War between Rome and the cities of Italy, whose inhabitants gain Roman citizenship.

**88–84**: the First Mithridatic War between Rome and Mithridates VI, king of Pontus.

**88**: Mithridates VI plunders Delos and massacres its inhabitants.

**75–63**: the Third Mithridatic War between Rome and Mithridates, king of Pontus.

**69**: Athenodoros, a pirate in Mithridates' pay, sacks Delos. The Roman legate Caius Triarius has a rampart erected there.

**67**: Pompey's war against the pirates.

# Introduction

During the second century and into the early first century BC, the island of Delos was home to the largest port of transit in the eastern Mediterranean. As such, it welcomed many Italian traders who prospered among its cosmopolitan population for some fifty or so years. The many buildings, statues, paintings and inscriptions* unearthed since 1873 by the French School at Athens have made it possible to trace out the life of this disparate yet influential community. It all began in 167 BC as part of the Roman conquest of the eastern Mediterranean. Having just vanquished the kingdom of Macedon, the Roman Senate rewarded its ally Athens by handing it Delos, a small but prosperous city thanks to its renowned sanctuary* of Apollo and its regional port of commerce. The Delians were driven from the island which was from then on inhabited and administered by the Athenians. In addition, in order to ruin its rival Rhodes, which at the time attracted the bulk of international trade, Rome made Delos a free port where merchant vessels were exonerated from import and export duties. In a few decades, as Rome continued its advance across the Greek world, Delos became the centre of trade between East and West. The destruction of Corinth in 146 and then the creation of the province of Asia in 129 BC made it an essential port-of-call for traders. And in a pirate-infested sea its inviolability was a further asset, since it was forbidden to be born or to die on this island that was consecrated entirely to Apollo.

In this highly conducive setting, Delos welcomed countless passing merchants and a large foreign population settled there beside the Athenians. Inscriptions tell us of Greeks from more or less remote cities, Egyptians, Phoenicians, Syrians, Jews, Samaritans, Arabs and, above all, very many Italians. At this time, the Italian economy was thriving and on the look-out for both a labour force and outlets for its agricultural produce. On Delos the Italian traders sold oil, wine and ceramics and bought slaves and various precious wares supplied by the Orientals. The island's new inhabitants were very quick to form ethnic associations but they also engaged in complex relations intermixing alliances and rivalries to ensure their economic and social success.

The city prospered and spread (1). New housing districts were built, sanctuaries were consecrated to foreign gods, the port and commercial infrastructures developed and the necropolis, on the island of Rheneia across the channel, became the last resting place of individuals from all over. The Italians were everywhere. After exploring the different facets of this particular group we shall set off on its tracks through the ruins and the museum of Delos.

(1)

# The Italians of Delos: a powerful community with many faces

## A COLOURFUL GROUP OPEN TO OTHER COMMUNITIES

More than 750 Italians have been counted from inscriptions. Although some of them sojourned on Delos from the end of the time of Delian independence and in the decades that followed the take-over by Athens in 167 BC, the vast majority settled there between 130 and 69 BC. They figure in the epitaphs*, the lists of subscribers* and the votive or honorific dedications*. Their origins and family ties can be ascertained from studying and categorizing their names (box 1).

Most of the Italians had a Latin name and came either from Rome or from Italian cities whose inhabitants, before the Social War (90–88 BC), did not generally have Roman citizenship (2). Although their nationality is seldom specified, the *nomen gentilicium** sometimes reveals the geographical origins of families. The Saufeii were well known in Praeneste (Latium) and the Granii in Puteoli (Campania), two flourishing cities that traded with Delos. Other families came from Apulia (Puglia), like the Gerillani, or were of Oscan origin (central Italy) like the Seii and the Stlaccii. But Greek names are also found when the Italians were from old Greek cities of the boot of Italy (Neapolis, Tarentum, Velia, Heraclea Lucania, etc.); they were then careful to specify their ethnic* to emphasize they belonged to the Italian community of Delos.

While some Italians were the isolated representatives of commercial houses based in Italy, most lived and worked as families. Some *gentes** were represented by 10 or even 15 or so individuals of varied status. In these families, there were often two or three free men, the family father and his son(s) or brother(s). They were accompanied by a few slaves or freedmen*, who were associated with their business or home life. Some probably came with them from Italy whereas others were acquired on the spot, but all had Greek or eastern names. The slaves of the Italians, or at least those we know from inscriptions, enjoyed particularly favourable circumstances. We find them paying for offerings* or contributing to subscriptions*, which means they had a *peculium** and some had funerary monuments similar to those of free men (3). Freedmen

**Greek names** have three components: first name, patronym (father's first name in the genitive) and ethnic (adjective formed from the name of the home city). e.g. *Apollonios Dioscouridou Neapolites*: Apollonios, son of Dioscourides, of Neapolis.

**Latin names** have four components: *praenomen* (first name), *nomen gentilicium* (family name), *patronym* (father's first name) and *cognomen* (nickname). The first name and patronym are always shortened and the *cognomen* is far from systematic. e.g. *P(ublius) Sexteilius L(ucii) f(ilius) Pilo*: Publius Sexteilius Pilo, son of Lucius.

Slaves and freedmen bore the *nomen gentilicium* of their master(s) or patron(s) and mention his (their) first name(s) by way of a patronym. Slaves invariably have a Greek first name. Once freed, they received a Latin *praenomen* but used their former slave first name as *cognomen*.
e.g. *Diodotus Seius C(aii) C(naeii) s(ervus)*: Diodotus Seius, slave of Caius and Cnaeus.
*C(aius) Seius Cn(aei) l(ibertus) Heracleo*: Caius Seius Heracleo, freedman of Cnaeus.

In Greek inscriptions, Latin names are transcribed into Greek characters and patronyms are put into the genitive, without any indication of status (son, freedman, slave). This makes it impossible to tell a free man from a freedman, since both have a Latin *praenomen*.
e.g. *Aulos Floueios Dekmou*: Aulus, son (or freedman) of Decimus.

In the lists of ephebes (and often also in the lists of subscribers), Roman names follow the pattern of Greek names, removing the *nomen gentilicium*, and sometimes indicate the ethnic *Romaios*, generically used to designate Italian origin and not Roman citizenship.
e.g. *Aulos Aulou Romaios*: Aulus, son of Aulus, Roman.

Women's names, attested only by their Greek transcription, are very varied. They often bear, as a first name, the feminized *nomen gentilicium* of their father, followed by the patronym (father's *praenomen*) or the *gamonym* (husband's *praenomen* and possibly *nomen gentilicium*). Some though have a real *praenomen*: the first names *Polla* and *Tertia* were particularly fashionable on Delos. Women seldom had a *cognomen*.
e.g. *Kaikilia Gnaiou*: Caecilia daughter of Cnaeus (Caecilius).
*Tertia Horaria Popliou Romaia Tryphera, gyne Popliou*: Tertia Oraria Tryphera, daughter of Publius and wife of Publius, Roman.

(1) *The names of the Italians of Delos*

The Italians on Delos

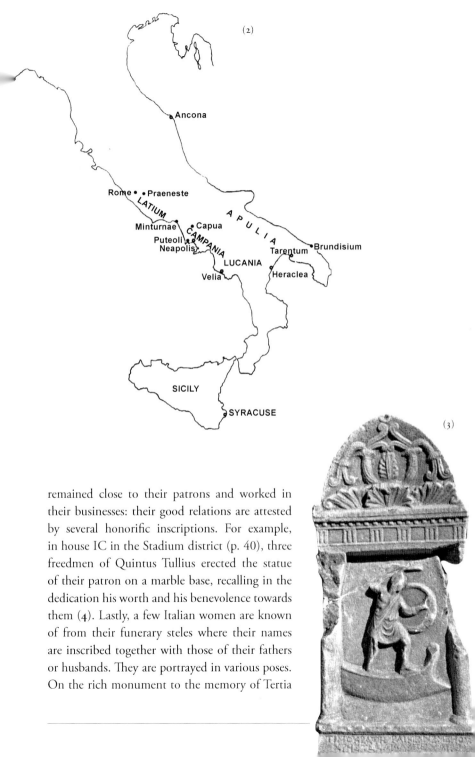

Ancona

Rome • • Praeneste

*LATIUM*

Minturnae • Capua

Puteoli

Neapolis

*CAMPANIA*

*A P U L I A*

Velia

*LUCANIA*

Tarentum • Brundisium

Heraclea

SICILY

SYRACUSE

(3)

remained close to their patrons and worked in their businesses: their good relations are attested by several honorific inscriptions. For example, in house IC in the Stadium district (p. 40), three freedmen of Quintus Tullius erected the statue of their patron on a marble base, recalling in the dedication his worth and his benevolence towards them (4). Lastly, a few Italian women are known of from their funerary steles where their names are inscribed together with those of their fathers or husbands. They are portrayed in various poses. On the rich monument to the memory of Tertia

Horaria (**5**), the deceased, sitting, holds the hand of a man, probably her husband Publius, while a small servant presents a jewellery box to her. Another stele depicts a young girl crouching, holding out a bunch of grapes to a small goose – the touching verse epitaph engraved beneath the carving tells us she was the daughter of a Roman citizen, Quintus Furius (**6** and box 2).

The Italian community therefore included individuals of diverse geographical origin, language, sex and status. When they came to settle on Delos, most of them were familiar, though, with Greek culture that was then a model in Rome and the main cities of the Italian peninsula. They spoke Greek and their

> I, a child citizen of Rome, Hades has called me and taken me away. In parting me from life, he has left my parents in exchange (for my loss) nothing but lamentations. My mother is called Artemisia, my father Quintus Furius. I am called by the same name my father bears. Sickness did not carry me off pitiably, I died without feeling any ill.

(2)   *Furia's epitaph* (SEG *47, 1232*)

inscriptions gave precedence to its use over Latin, at least in private settings. They were very much open to the Greek and Oriental populations they rubbed shoulders with in many places on the island.

Thus Italians are seen to have attended the gymnasium, a place given over to sport, intellectual teaching and sociability, open to various age groups. Initially located in the building now known as the 'Lake Palaestra', the gymnasium was transferred by the Athenians near to the stadium in the north-east of the island ⑭ in the early first century BC (**7**). Italian names appear on the official lists, the dedications and the graffiti engraved on the marble benches. The young men aged 18 to 20 years were included

in the *ephebeia**. In 119/18 BC a list of ephebes* comprises five Italians, six Athenians and twenty-nine other Greeks and Orientals, giving some idea of the numerical size of the foreign population.

The population also gathered at the island's many sanctuaries, some dedicated for centuries to the Greek divinities and others created more recently in honour of foreign gods. The immensely successful sanctuaries of the Egyptian gods Serapis, Isis, Anubis and Harpocrates (Horus) and the Syrian gods Hadad and Atargatis were administered by Athens, which saw to their upkeep, appointed the cultual personnel and organized the religious festivals (⑰, ⑱, ⑲). The Italians, like many other foreigners, were faithful devotees of these oriental divinities to whom they made countless offerings. On the lists of subscribers to Egyptian sanctuaries we count seventy Italians, including many slaves, both men and women. The example of the Aemilii family is instructive: in 112/11 BC, Lucius Aemilius, son or freedman of Publius, together with another Italian, Aulus Gessius, dedicated a *pastophorion** and its furnishing to the Egyptian gods in their own names and those of their wives and children; in 106/05, a slave, Hellas Aemilia, consecrated a statuette to the Egyptian gods in her name and in the name of Sappho and Spurius (her comrades?); in 90, Publius Aemilius, son of Lucius, Roman, offered an *exedra** to the Syrian gods in his name and that of his son Publius. Let us finally list Spurius Stertinius who made two offerings to the Egyptian gods, one to the Nymphs, one to the Charites and two to Artemis Soteira (8): this Italian was plainly drawn more to the eastern and Greek cults than to those of his homeland.

Down the decades, the Italians therefore mixed with the cosmopolitan population, adopting the same beliefs and behaviours, in a sort of great Delian cultural melting pot. This integration was manifested also by bonds of friendship and matrimonial alliances with other communities. We see Italians consorting with Athenians to make common dedications: the Italian Gorgias, son of Damoxenos, from Heraclea Lucania and the Athenian Ariston, son of Gorgias, together erected the honorific statues of their friends Aulus and Publius Gabinii, Roman magistrates. Even more surprisingly, four Italian freedmen joined with the famed Athenian Dionysios, son of Nikon, who had served as *epimeletes* of the island*,

to dedicate a monument. Several cases of mixed marriages are also suspected, even if the interpretation of names mixing Latin and Greek elements remains intricate. Thus Caius Seius Aristomachus was the son of a Roman citizen, Cnaeus Seius, and of Cleopatra, daughter of Philostratos, of Arados in Phoenicia. He bears the Roman *nomen gentilicium* of his father, a Roman *praenomen* and a Greek *cognomen*. He and his mother remained faithful to the cult of the Syrian gods, as attested by two dedications. It is likely that marriages between Italians and Orientals, much like the friendships displayed in the dedications, concealed economic or even political interests.

Such interests prompted some Orientals to join the Italian community by obtaining citizenship of the Greek cities of southern Italy. The most famous case is that of the banker Philostratos, son of Philostratos. This figure, whose family is known from thirteen inscriptions,

(8)

was from Ascalon in Palestine and settled on Delos with his wife, two sons (at least one of whom was an ephebe) and his slave Chaireas. Faithful to the gods of his homeland, to whom he made several dedications at the sanctuary of the divinities of Ascalon, on Mount Kynthos (16), he soon obtained the citizenship of Neapolis, probably through his ties with Italian traders and his generosity towards them. Evidence of this is a dedication of three Egnatii brothers who raised a statue to him, calling him an *euergetes**, and two others from groupings of Italian, Athenian and foreign merchants. We shall see that Philostratos was one of the most generous donors to the Agora of the Italians (pp. 49–50) and that the acquisition of his Neapolitan citizenship was prompted by his business needs, since the Italians monopolized banking.

## AN INFLUENTIAL ASSOCIATION: THE *ITALICI*

Foreigners from all backgrounds, then, met at various venues, entering into business arrangements, possibly reinforced by matrimonial alliances. Even so each community was careful to maintain and even strengthen its internal bonds through religious, cultural and/or commercial associations. The associations of Orientals are the best known. For example, the '*koinon**  of the Poseidoniasts of Berytos, merchants, shippers, and warehousemen' brought together Phoenician merchants from what is modern Beirut. They had a clubhouse (9) built in the northern district (12) comprising a peristyle (F), an assembly room (E), shrines* for the ancestral gods (V) and warehousing facilities (J–Q). The members of the association, who paid an annual contribution, complied with a *nomos* (rules and regulations) and met periodically in assemblies to vote on decrees and elect a president, a secretary and treasurers.

The inscriptions we have are unfortunately not specific about the organization of the Italians and historians have long debated the nature and purposes of their grouping(s). It seems there were both business associations grouping Italian businessmen by activity – we shall come back to them – and a religious and cultural association, called *Italici* in Latin and *Italoi* in Greek (The Italians) that united all individuals from the peninsula. This association was based at two central points on the island, the ancient names of which are unknown: 'the Agora of the Competaliasts' (1), a public square by the port, was home to its shrines and 'the Agora of the Italians' (8), on the northern side of the sanctuary of Apollo, was a gigantic place for gathering and pageantry.

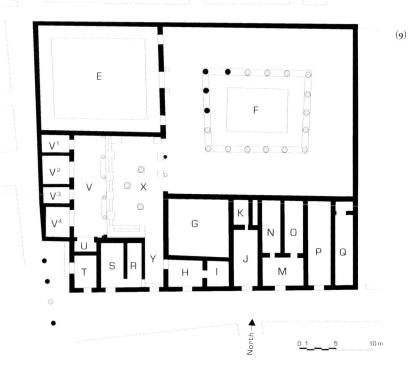

No administrative documents from the *Italici* have been preserved but the association's name appears in several honorific dedications. For example, it paid tribute to one of its most eminent members, Caius Ofellius Ferus, by erecting a marble likeness of him in a niche* of the Agora of the Italians (10). The dedication engraved on the base states: 'The *Italici* have consecrated to Apollo the statue of Caius Ofellius Ferus son of Marcus for his fairness and benevolence towards them.' As we shall see, the association of the *Italici* received dedications too: all of the porticoes of the Agora of the Italians were devoted 'to Apollo and to the *Italici*' by its members or its representatives. It is probable that, like the Poseidoniasts of Berytos, the *Italici* adhered to a rule, organized assemblies and elected officials tasked with administering and representing their community. A score of dedications, mostly bilingual, come from colleges* of five to twelve Italians bearing the titles of *magistri*\* in Latin and of *Hermaistai, Apolloniastai, Poseidoniastai* and *Kompetaliastai* in Greek (11 and box 3). These *magistri*, who addressed their dedications to the Italian gods and to the *Italici*, may not have been the association's only dignitaries but they were plainly designated to manage its shrines. Categorization of the inscriptions informs us about the four

(11)

colleges, each devoted to one or more Graeco-Roman divinities: the *magistri* of Mercury (Hermes), known as *Hermaistai* (Hermaists) in Greek, revered the god of commerce and his mother Maia, an ancient Italic goddess; the *magistri* of Neptune (Poseidon), or *Poseidoniastai* (Poseidoniasts), honoured the god of sea-faring; the *magistri* of Apollo, or *Apolloniastai* (Apolloniasts), worshipped the island's leading god; and the *Kompetaliastai* (Competaliasts), whose Latin name is not attested since all of the inscriptions preserved are in Greek, venerated the Lares Compitales, Roman divinities of the streets and crossroads. If the dates of certain inscriptions are to be believed, these colleges were renewed periodically, probably each year. We do not know by what criteria they were chosen but it has been observed that the same person could belong to two different colleges: the freedman Aulus Cerrinius was a Competaliast and a Hermaist in turn. Often several members of the same family held office in the same college whether in the same year or in succession: among the Paconii, we know of four Competaliasts and two Hermaists, Apolloniasts or Poseidoniasts. Belonging to a college was certainly a source of prestige and influence, but it also required a certain degree of wealth. The *magistri* made many costly offerings (statues, altars or temples) either during their year of office or after leaving office: in

(10)

(12)

Publius Sextilius Pilo, son of Lucius
Caius Crassicius, son of Publius
Marcus Audius, son of Marcus
Marcus Cottius, son of Numerius
Cnaeus Tutorius, son of Cnaeus
Numerius Stenius, son of Marcus
Publius Arellius, freedman of Quintus
Tiberius Seius, freedman of Marcus
Numerius Tutorius, freedman of Cnaeus
Quintus Nummius, freedman of Lucius
Decimus Maecius, freedman of Lucius
Publius Castricius, freedman of Publius,
(being) *magistri* of Mercury, Apollo and
Neptune, have had (this statue) made and dedicated it
to Hercules, under the consulate of Cnaeus Papirius
and Caius Caecilius.

(3)  *Dedication of the Hermaists, Apolloniasts and
Poseidoniasts to Heracles in 113 BC (ID 1753)*

the former case, the offerings were probably financed by the association (a single dedication specifies they made the offering 'at their own expense') but in the latter case, these were acts of euergetism*.

However, the make-up of the colleges complied with a strict rule: the Hermaists, Apolloniasts and Poseidoniasts were all free men, whether by birth or by emancipation, whereas the Competaliasts were slaves and a few freedmen. Now, in Italy, the cult of the Lares Compitales was traditionally ministered by slaves. It is likely that the creation of the college of Competaliasts served two purposes: to rally the Italians around an emblematic cult of their region of origin but also to incorporate within their community slaves of Greek and eastern origin, some of whom were ignorant of their masters' traditions. Being a Competaliast allowed them to serve in an official capacity and climb the social ladder, in an economic context where there were many opportunities for enrichment and emancipation. However, the free-born Italians saw to it that precedence was maintained: although freedmen were listed in the colleges of the Hermaists, Apolloniasts and Poseidoniasts, they invariably came at the end of the rolls; in addition, the three colleges of free men made joint dedications but never mixed with the Competaliasts; lastly, as shall be seen, the latter were confined to the Agora of the Competaliasts and no slaves featured among the donors of the Agora of the Italians.

Four main cults were taken charge of by the *magistri*, who also made dedications to secondary gods. Their divinities bore a Roman name in the Latin inscriptions but they are usually attested by their Greek name.

Mercury (Hermes) and Maia were worshiped in two shrines on the Agora of the Competaliasts ⓵ (pp. 28–36). On the same square, the Competaliasts venerated the Lares Compitales, protectors of the crossroads (*compita*): unknown to the Greeks (hence the name of *theoi*, 'the gods', for them in Greek), they were twin gods, depicted as two young men dressed in tunics and dancing face to face holding a rhyton* (**12**). The Italian families also paid private reverence to them on altars built at the doors to their houses on the annual festival of the *Compitalia* (pp. 44–47).

It does not seem that the *Italici* built a shrine to Neptune (Poseidon) but they worshipped him in the *Poseideion* ⓾, the Athenian sanctuary on the Agora of Theophrastos: the dedications of the *magistri* to Poseidon came from this area, and a Latin graffito, engraved on the altar of Poseidon by one Caius Nerius, is addressed to several Greek and Italian gods (Eros, Apollo, Jupiter, Neptune, Minerva and Mercury).

Only a single dedication of the Apolloniasts to the island's main god is preserved. It is not impossible that they were tasked with offering an ox in the name of the association of the *Italici* at the Athenian festival of the *Apollonia*, as was the case of the *boutrophoi* ('ox-rearers') of the Poseidoniasts of Berytos.

Lastly, various divinities attested by inscriptions of the Competaliasts or depicted in paintings at the doors of houses were part of the pantheon of the Italians: Hercules (Heracles), Minerva (Athena), Dionysos, Jupiter Liber (Zeus Eleutherios) and the personifications Pistis (Good faith) and Rome.

The association of the *Italici* therefore had both a religious calling, allowing the Italians to engage in joint worship to their gods, and a social one: it is to be imagined as a 'club' of sorts that facilitated encounters and mutual support among its members, strengthening and regulating their ties, whatever their geographical and social background. Accordingly, rivalries and tensions were to

be found among this disparate group. Evidence of this is a copper curse tablet*
found in the necropolis of Rheneia, on which one Titus Paconius cursed in Latin
twenty-one of his enemies, most of them Italians and four of them members
of his own family (box 4)!

However, the association had a political goal too. While it encouraged sociability
among its members, it sought above all to show itself as the island's most powerful
community. The Italians, who were very numerous, had the asset of the (at least
symbolic) patronage of Rome, which had handed Delos over to the Athenians
and continued to carry weight in the island's political, religious and economic
life. The *Italici* maintained excellent relations with the Roman magistrates who
stopped off at Delos: besides Caius Julius Caesar's ties with the oil merchants
to which we shall return, mention can be made of Lucius Munatius Plancus,
honoured in 88 BC at the Agora of the Italians by 'the *Italici* and the Greeks
who commerce on Delos' or again Caius Billienus, who received, when he was
legate, a statue from 'those who do business on Delos' and another, as proconsul*
of Asia, from his friend Midas son of Zeno, of Heraclea Lucania (13).

For this reason, in the joint dedications that the population regularly offered to the
Athenian and Roman magistrates, the Italians were named in second place after
the Athenians and before the other foreigners. This was the case on the base of the
statue of the *epimeletes* of the island Theophrastos (14), raised by 'the Athenians,
the Romans and the other foreigners resident on and passing through Delos'.
Behind the name 'Romans' were not just the *Italici* but also a wider group including
Italian traders and *naukleroi** who stopped off on the island: although they were far
from all Roman citizens, they preferred to refer to themselves as such in order to

(A curse upon) Lucius Paconius the Elder, Quintus Tullius son of Quintus,
[...], Numerius Cottius son of Numerius [---], Caius Seius Cheilo son
of Caius, [---]ius Aristomachus, Caecilius son of Lucius [---], Quintus
Samiarius Ar[---] son of Marcus, Manius Satricanius Ar[---], Aulus and
Quintus Paconii sons of Marcus, Heracleides, Antipatrus, [---], Heliodorus,
[---]TIV[---], Demetrius, Caius, Seuthes the jurist, Serapion son of Serapion,
Publius Granius Alexandrus, [---]tius Aeg[---] son of Decimus, [---]cius
Neiceporus, Cnaeus Paconius Apolloni[us], the Mari(i) Gerrillanni [---],
Nemerius and Marcus Raii, and any other who shall be an enemy for
Titus Paconius!

(4)   *Curse tablet of Rheneia* (ID 2534)

The Italians of Delos: a powerful community with many faces

display their proximity with Roman power. Similarly, a strategic use of Latin can be observed in the official inscriptions of the *Italici*: while Greek was the language common to the island's entire population and the Italians used it systematically in private, the *magistri* in office drew up bilingual dedications as if to underscore the specificity of their ethnic group. Lastly, to date their inscriptions, they mentioned not just the Athenian *epimeletes* of the island but also the consuls*, as another way of recalling their connection with the Roman state (box 3).

We are therefore dealing with a highly organized and influential group, out to promote its members' social success and economic prosperity, but which benefitted therefrom too.

(14)

## LUCRATIVE BUSINESSES: COMMERCE AND BANKING

Besides their geographical origins, the Italians were united by common business interests. Their main if not their only activity was commerce. Like the other inhabitants of Delos, they are presented in the joint dedications as *emporoi*, long-distance traders who imported and exported goods, *naukleroi*, owners of the ships that provided the transport, or *trapezitai*, that is, bankers.

We know little of the shipowners and of the transporting of goods. Little is known of the port and no wreck has so far been excavated in the approaches to Delos. However, graffiti on the stuccoed walls of Delian houses depict, apart from many warships, a few merchant vessels (15). At this time, these were round hulled vessels, on average 15–25 m and sometimes up to 40 m

long. Although the inscriptions tell us of no shipowners among the *Italici*, a fragmentary dedication comes from at least two Italian sailors, addressing the saviour Dioscuri\*, in their name and the name of the *ploizomenoi* (seafarers): they had probably survived a shipwreck. Others were less fortunate: the funerary stele of the Roman Spurius Granius, son (or freedman) of Aulus, shows a man sitting forlorn on a rock watching a vessel in distress with three passengers on board (**16**). This type of representation, recurrent on Rheneia, was chosen for the cenotaphs\* of the shipwrecked.

Cicero's second speech against Verres in 70 BC refers to the merchandise confiscated from the Italian traders arriving from the Orient in Sicily: 'some brought him purple from Tyr, others brought incense, perfumes and linen garments; several of them jewels and pearls; some of them Greek wines or slaves bought in Asia, so that, from the items of their trade, one might judge the places from whence they came.' Although it does not concern Delos specifically, this passage gives an idea of the products that the Italians came there to get from eastern merchants. Slaves were undoubtedly the largest part of the cargoes, if the geographer Strabo is to be believed: 'They found a great rich market place, that of Delos, that could take in and sell off several thousand slaves a day, hence the often-quoted saying: Jump to it, merchant, berth, offload, it's all sold.' However, no Delian inscription mentions these various trades.

We are, though, well informed about the products carried to Delos by the Italians: mostly oil and wine with, as a supplement to the cargoes of amphorae, Italian ceramics. The oil merchants in particular had founded a business association that bore their name (*Olearii* in Latin and *Elaipolai* in Greek) and had placed themselves under the protection of Hercules (Heracles) and Mercury (Hermes) to whom they had consecrated a small temple. Their headquarters was probably on the *emporion*\*, south of the Agora of the Competaliasts ① where two dedications have been discovered (p. 37): one, on a statue base, is a tribute from

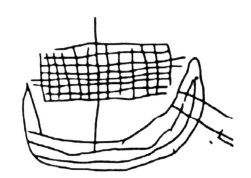

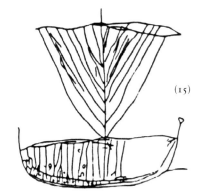

(15)

The Italians on Delos

the *Olearii* to the proconsul Caius Julius Caesar (father and namesake of the famous dictator), who governed the Roman province of Asia at the beginning of the first century BC. The other is the name of the same magistrate engraved on a *sekoma** that he undoubtedly presented to them (**17**): this marble table, the holed basin of which was formerly topped by a bronze cylinder, served for measuring out volumes of oil at the time of sale. It should be concluded from this that the *Olearii* had close ties with the Roman authorities, particularly as this gift from the proconsul was made further to a law of Athens altering weights and measures so as to facilitate conversion between the Athenian and Roman systems.

The Italian oil came mostly from the south of the peninsula and was transported in globular amphorae known as 'Brindisian amphorae', a number of which have been discovered on Delos (**18a**): some were for the resident population and the remainder redistributed around the eastern Mediterranean. Similarly, the wine trade is attested by a single dedication from wine merchants (*Oinopolai* in Greek) and an impressive number of Italian wine amphorae. Two types prevail as in many sites in the eastern Mediterranean: the Lamboglia 2, from the Adriatic coast, and the Dressel 1A and 1C, from the Tyrrhenian coast (**18b–d**). In a warehouse district north-east of the Agora of the Italians some sixty amphorae were discovered *in situ*, all of Italian origin, lodged in the ground and for some still capped by a plaster-sealed ceramic lid. This was plainly a warehouse where the *negotiatores* stored wine imported from Italy.

Apart from commerce, banking seems to have been in Italian hands. Other than Philostratos of Ascalon, who managed to join the community of the *Italici* by becoming a citizen of Neapolis (p. 13), we know of no Greek or Oriental bankers on Delos. The bankers took in deposits of money, engaged in foreign exchange operations and lent money at interest: they therefore played a major role in the Delian *emporion*. This is why they were honoured on several occasions: in

(**17**)

The Italians of Delos: a powerful community with many faces

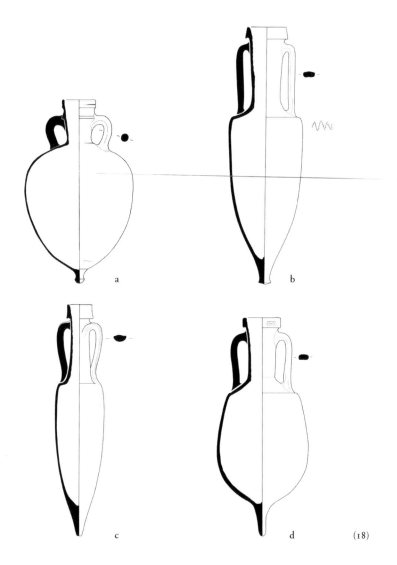

a     b     c     d     (18)

the late second and early first centuries, the banker Marius Gerillanus son of Marius was presented with three statues by different groups of Greek and Italian traders celebrating his merits and his qualities as a good man. It is amusing to observe that he was not unanimously acclaimed since he was also cursed by Titus Paconius in the tablet of Rheneia (box 4).

The Italians on Delos

Another banker, Marcus Minatius, son of Sextus, is well known from the honorific decree voted for him by the Poseidoniasts of Berytos in 149/48 BC. The Phoenician association had borrowed a large amount from him to build their clubhouse (9) and were looking for funds to complete it. Minatius waived the interest on the sum already loaned and even offered another 7000 drachmas. One might wonder about the reasons for such generosity, which attests to the prosperity of the Italian banker in the early decades of the rise of the Delian *emporion*: he probably already did business with the merchants of Berytos and so hoped to strengthen his collaboration with them by becoming a full member of their association. To thank him, the association did indeed offer him numerous honours and advantages: a crown, a statue, a painted effigy, the offering of an ox in his name at the *Apollonia*, exemption from any financial contribution and the right to bring one or two guests of his choice to the festivals in honour of the ancestral gods.

The Italian bankers probably did business on the ancient Agora of the Delians ③, which took the name of 'Tetragon' after the agora* was transferred to the Agora of Theophrastos ⑨ (**19**). On this square flanked by porticoes, whose offices and shops were leased out by the Athenian administration, three dedications in honour of Italian bankers have been discovered. But they also

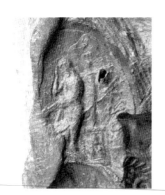

had offices in their homes where they kept deeds and contracts concerning their own affairs or those of other individuals. The 'House of the Seals' (13), destroyed by fire in 69 BC, may have been the home of two Italian bankers. Nearly 15,000 clay tags were collected there bearing some 26,000 imprints of seals* from documents drawn up on papyri. Some sixty imprints bore the names of Italians (20). Also collected from the rubble were fragments of marble busts (21) providing striking portraits of two mature men, bare chested with a cloak thrown over their shoulder in the manner of Caius Ofellius (10), of stern or even haughty appearance. It is tempting to recognize in them two Italians who owned the house and whose business was clearly prosperous.

This picture of the activities of the Italians on Delos will have shown how lucrative their commerce was. More than all the other communities, they used

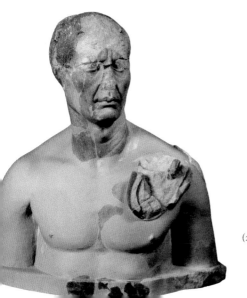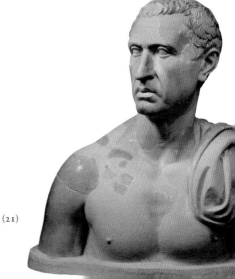

(21)

their wealth to promote their image, constantly advertising their presence in the Delian landscape. We have already mentioned several times their offerings to the Italian and foreign divinities and the honorific statues they financed individually or collectively. We should add their recurrent participation in the construction of buildings which were acts of euergetism: just as Marcus Minatius contributed to the building of the Clubhouse of the Poseidoniasts of Berytos, it was Italians who financed, by tranches, all of the Agora of the Italians. As shall be seen the eight porticoes, the *exedrae* and the *laconicum** of the *thermae* (22) bore the names of the people or groups who had them built. Among these featured in good position *magistri* after they had left office. So we see a form of outbidding in gifts that was both emulation within the Italian community and a common and probably well thought-out strategy of occupation of space. This is why the Italians were the only foreigners of whom we find traces in many of the public or private buildings with religious, economic or social purposes.

(22)

The Italians of Delos: a powerful community with many faces

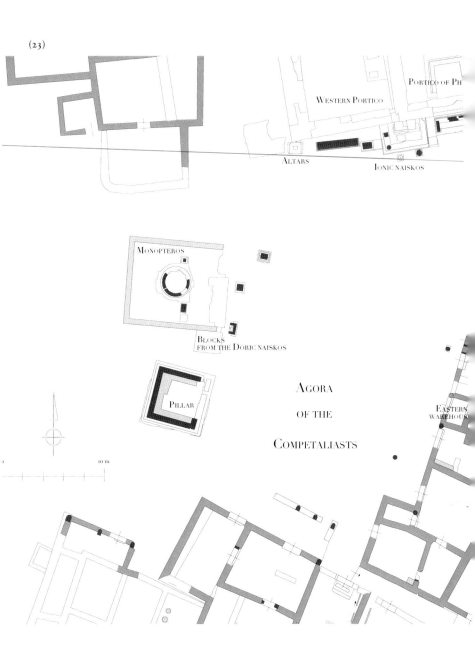

(23)

PORTICO OF PH

WESTERN PORTICO

ALTARS

IONIC NAISKOS

MONOPTEROS

BLOCKS
FROM THE DORIC NAISKOS

PILLAR

AGORA

OF THE

COMPETALIASTS

EASTERN
WAREHOUSE

10 m

# The haunts of the Italians: from neighbourhood shrines to ostentatious monuments

*The places where Italians lived shall be presented in both a thematic and geographical order. The italicized passages suggest a visit of about 90 minutes (excluding the occasional detours indicated). The necropolis of Rheneia is off bounds and shall not be discussed but some of the Italian funerary steles may be contemplated in Mykonos Archaeological Museum.*

## THE AGORA OF THE COMPETALIASTS AND THE OFFICIAL SHRINES OF THE *ITALICI*

Leaving the mole, the first remains encountered are those of a public square where the Italians established their shrines ①. Archaeologists have called it the 'Agora of the Competaliasts' (**23** and **53**) or 'Agora of the Hermaists' because of the many dedications by the *magistri* found there. However, its ancient name remains unknown.

This vast paved esplanade was built by filling a coastal marsh as part of the port's development by the *epimeletes* of the island Theophrastos shortly before 125 BC. It was at the heart of the *emporion*, the port zone reserved for international trade, which extended from the Western Portico to the bay south of the Warehouse with Columns. The shoreline has been greatly altered since Antiquity by the rise in relative sea level of about 2.50 m and the creation of the modern mole with the rubble from excavation. In the second century BC, the port seems to have been composed of a shallow harbour, fringed by a beach where small boats were hauled up whereas the larger ones remained in the anchorage. This harbour lay to the north-west of the Agora of the Competaliasts that was probably, like today, the main landing stage of the island and the *emporion*. It goes to show how influential the *Italici* were: whereas the other communities worshipped their gods in private buildings, the *Italici* had secured authorization to build shrines in the middle of a busy public square, exhibiting their gods, their prestigious offerings and their engraved names to everyone's gaze.

The Agora of the Competaliasts, an inescapable transit point, formed the cross-roads of several streets: on the sea front, one led north to the Agora of Theophrastos ⑨, where local commerce was conducted, and the other south to the shops and warehouses of the *emporion* ②. To the north-east, one could go via Porticoes Street either to the sanctuary of Apollo or to the Tetragon (Agora of the Delians ③). To the east, two streets led to the town's southern residential districts and to the theatre. The square was hemmed to the north by the short side of two back-to-back porticoes: the Western Portico, facing the port, was for trading and accommodated the *epimeletes* of the *emporion*, the Athenian magistrate who supervised transit trade; the Portico of Philip, along the Dromos (sacred way) leading to the sanctuary of Apollo, was more of a shaded walk. On the other two sides of the square can be observed the walls of housing blocks (*insulae*) where shops were located. Those of the eastern façade opened onto a modest portico now walled up, whose miscellaneous columns supported a protruding upper storey. To the south, the houses lined by two porticoes of marble half-column pillars were built out onto the esplanade in the imperial period. Lastly, in the centre of the square, a foundation with marble steps supported a monumental pillar some 10 m tall, probably for the statue of a Roman magistrate in a chariot (see **33**). Apart from this exceptional offering and a few bases and *exedrae*, all the monuments on the square were dedicated by Italian *magistri*.

**The Ionic naiskos\* of the Hermaists**, built against the walled part of the Western Portico and the Portico of Philip, to the north of the square, was consecrated to the Roman god Mercury (Hermes in Greek) and his mother, the nymph Maia. Only its foundation is preserved (**24**) but the two steps of the crepis\* are easily recognizable on which there remain, on the left side, the lower part of a column and of an anta. On and around the monument lie other blocks that indicate a prostyle\* baldachin with four columns of the Ionic or Corinthian order, no capital having been preserved (**25**). The fragment of the dedication engraved on the architrave\* tells us the temple was built by a college of six Hermaists. Inside we notice the plinths of the two bases for the statues of Mercury and Maia, which were protected by marble barriers between the columns. In front of the naiskos stand, on the right, a cylindrical altar decorated with garlands and *bucrania\**, and on the left a marble offertory box dedicated by Caius Varius, freedman of Caius. The box has a slot through which the faithful deposited money. Offerings were recovered by lifting the drum section that was hollowed

The Italians on Delos

out and separable from its square base; it is decorated with two snakes carved in the marble and a bronze caduceus, the attributes of Mercury (26). Visible traces on the first step of the crepis show that other offerings, probably small statue bases, had been sealed there too.

In the centre of the square, **the monopteros\* of the Competaliasts** was a temple of the Lares Compitales, Roman divinities of the crossroads. Unlike the naiskos of Mercury and Maia, which opened directly onto the esplanade, it was surrounded by a peribolos, a low stone wall once stuccoed, bounding a rectangular platform standing proud of the paving (27). The temple was of a form unique on Delos and still extremely rare at the time, that of a circular marble monopteros housing the cult statues (28). Only a single base, deposited on the crepis, remains of the four columns and it is impossible to determine whether they were of Ionic or Corinthian order. The conical roof was decorated with a scale motif, a model that was to be highly successful later in the Roman world. There must have been a square ceiling slab resting on the straight cornices behind the entablature\* blocks, the weight of which offset the large cantilever of the upper part of the edifice over the columns. This monopteros, which is outstanding in its shape and architectural technique, is distinctive in not having the richly carved decoration that generally characterizes structures of this kind.

The fragmentary dedication, inscribed on the architrave, comes from five freedmen and a slave, all Italians, who must have made up a college of Competaliasts. An inscription naming the same individuals was engraved on a fragment of the base that supported the statues of the Lares Compitales within the monopteros. Lastly, a small altar from a monolithic block of marble, now laid along the Western Portico, must have stood before the temple (28 and 29): it is sculpted with a (hammered) relief representing the twin gods, face to face, raising a leg in a dance and holding a laurel branch over their shoulder. The inscription engraved between the Lares recalls the simultaneous consecration of the altar, the temple and the divine statues. North and south of the monopteros, three statue bases also bear dedications of the Competaliasts.

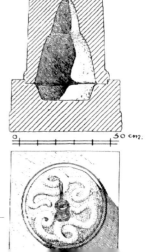

(26)

(29)

**The Doric naiskos of the Hermaists**, of which only seven fragments of the entablature remain, belonged to a third Italian shrine (30 and 31). On its architrave, now laid on a masonry foundation south of the monopteros, we can read the bilingual dedication of a college of Hermaists to Mercury (Hermes) and Maia. As these blocks were discovered on the Agora of the Competaliasts, it is likely that the edifice was there but its foundation has vanished either because of the rise in sea level or buried beneath the later dwellings that encroached on the esplanade.

On the Agora of the Competaliasts and in particular along the Western Portico, we can also observe **the altars and bases of statues** offered by the Hermaists and Competaliasts. These offerings probably came from the three shrines but they are so plentiful that some may have been in place on the esplanade (33). The abridged dedications engraved on the altars indicate that the *magistri* were in the habit of consecrating an altar and a statue at the same time to varied divinities such as Heracles, Athena or Maia. The bronze statues whose feet were embedded and sealed with lead in the cavities carved in the upper surfaces of the bases, were of varied dimensions: to the east of the monopteros, a large base of the Hermaists bore a human-sized statue of Mercury whereas the same god must have measured at most 80 cm on a small monolithic base at the north of the square. The cylindrical altars set on moulded plinths are decorated with garlands and *bucrania* according to a model commonly found on Delos and Rheneia: in particular, at the north of the esplanade is that of Heracles made of blue marble (32) and that of Athena made of pink marble.

These many offerings are evidence less of the Italians' devotion to their national gods than of their concern for prestigious display. It is striking that all the

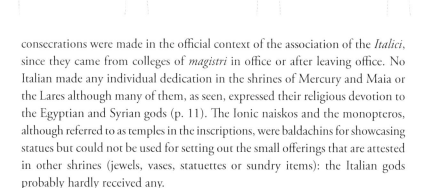

consecrations were made in the official context of the association of the *Italici*, since they came from colleges of *magistri* in office or after leaving office. No Italian made any individual dedication in the shrines of Mercury and Maia or the Lares although many of them, as seen, expressed their religious devotion to the Egyptian and Syrian gods (p. 11). The Ionic naiskos and the monopteros, although referred to as temples in the inscriptions, were baldachins for showcasing statues but could not be used for setting out the small offerings that are attested in other shrines (jewels, vases, statuettes or sundry items): the Italian gods probably hardly received any.

The rites are not known. Much as the Phoenician association of the Poseidoniasts of Berytos had created an annual festival for its eponymous god, the *Poseidonia*, it is likely that the *Italici* celebrated *Hermaia* each year in honour of Mercury and Maia in the two shrines of the Agora of the Competaliasts: it might be imagined there was a procession and a sacrifice by the *magistri* before the naiskos, but no sources confirm this. However, the festival of the *Compitalia* in honour of the Lares Compitales is documented by many pictures discovered in houses and warehouses, to which we shall return: although the sacrifices shown were made in a private setting, it may be that *ludi\** were held on the esplanade of the Agora of the Competaliasts.

(33)

## THE SEAFRONT WAREHOUSES AND THE OIL AND WINE BUSINESS

*From the Agora of the Competaliasts, we head south along the seafront where we come almost immediately to Warehouses α (alpha). β (beta) and γ (gamma)* ② *which were places for sale and storage in the* emporion.

These commercial buildings surely housed the headquarters of the *Olearii*, the association of Italian oil merchants, although it is not known exactly where: the *sekoma* of C. Julius Caesar (**17**) and his statue base (pp. 21–23) have been discovered, the one on the street in front of Warehouses β and γ and the other in a shop north of Warehouse α. The single dedication of the wine merchants (p. 23) also comes from this sector.

Warehouses α, β and γ are laid out identically (**34**). Through a central vestibule, we enter a large paved inner courtyard that on three sides served spacious rooms, some with windows. In Warehouses β and γ (**35**), the courtyard was lined with marble columned porticoes which, upstairs, gave access to other rooms

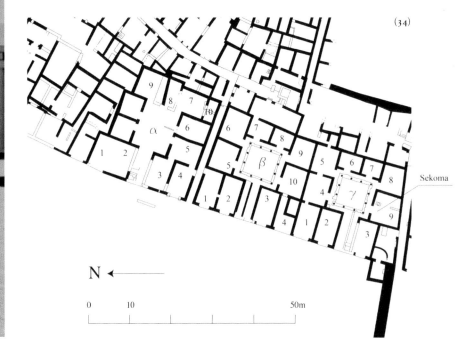

(34)

Sekoma

N ◂

0   10   50m

of the same size. These were independent of the ground floor and served by a wooden staircase in a long corridor parallel to the vestibule. On the warehouse frontage, other rooms opened onto the street through large bays: some had two doorsteps, one for the ground floor and the other for a staircase leading to an upstairs room. Examination of the holes cut in the sills reveals that each room had been fitted with a succession of various types of doors – the Ancient Greeks took their doors with them when they moved. So these were buildings whose numerous premises were planned to be independent with the possibility of attributing them to different people and purposes.

In each of the three warehouses, a *sekoma* has been found for measuring out large quantities of liquids: the only one that is intact, and strictly identical to that of C. Julius Caesar (p. 23), is to be found in room 9 of Warehouse γ. It is a marble table, formerly set on legs, with a hemispherical cavity into which a probably graduated metal cylinder was fitted. The outlet was stopped before the oil or wine was poured in. Once measured, it was allowed to flow out into a container placed under the table. A small circular indent was designed to collect any overflow. This *sekoma*, like the other three, bears a dedication of Ariarathes, *epimeletes* of the *emporion*, tasked with overseeing that transactions in the port of commerce were right and proper. It is likely therefore that Warehouses α, β and γ accommodated, under the supervision of the Athenian city, the oil and wine merchants and served as their offices, and as places for storage and wholesale transactions.

*After visiting the seafront warehouses, we go along the street between Warehouses α and β, then turn along the first street on the left and the second on the right. This leads to a winding path that can be followed eastwards to the Aphrodision and then the House of the Herm ⒋.*

## THE HOUSES OF THE ITALIANS AND THE FESTIVAL OF THE *COMPITALIA*

While it is easy to recognize the official shrines of the *Italici* on Delos and to guess at their presence in the warehouses of the *emporion*, it is far more complex to look for their traces in private houses. Yet no Greek site offers as rich and varied remains of dwellings as Delos. At the time the island became Athenian and the first foreigners settled there, the houses were concentrated to the south of the sanctuary of Apollo, on the hill of the theatre and in the Inopos valley. Because of the growth in population, new residential districts were built to the north and east of the sanctuary and on the eastern shore, below the stadium. In the old and recent sectors alike, the luxurious decoration of certain houses is evidence of the enrichment of the inhabitants but, barring a few rare exceptions, it is impossible to ascertain their nationality. The foreigners were not grouped by districts and the architectural uniformity of the houses in no way reflects the cosmopolitanism of the inhabitants, whose activities, cults and lifestyles, as seen, were very much alike. Moreover, all the evidence is that the populations mixed and mutually influenced each other: while the Italians imported a few architectural or decorative features from their homeland, these were soon copied and the occurrence, for example, of a Campanian peristyle* in the House of the Tritons does not necessarily mean that its occupants were Italian. Allowance

should also be made for the fact that houses changed hands and in many instances Italians inherited buildings designed by others.

And yet there are a few tell-tale clues from which to identify Italian houses. In some dwellings, dedications from Italians reveal that they occupied the premises at some point. In the vestibule of House E on East Street ⑥, a dedication from Spurius Stertinius to Artemis Soteira is set in masonry in a niche where the statuette of the goddess, now vanished, once rested (36). The dwelling where this character, well known for his religious devotion (pp. 11–12), once lived is modest: a few rooms of various sizes open onto a paved courtyard with no peristyle or decoration. House IC of the Stadium district ⑮ belonged at one time to the Tullii family: two marble bases from the upper floor were collected from the rubble, one with a bilingual dedication of three freedmen to their patron Quintus Tullius (p. 9 and 4). Outside, on either side of the entrance, the discovery of a remarkable set of religious paintings of the *Compitalia* confirms the occupants' nationality (37): we shall return to this. But let us head first for the wealthy home of the Paconii, in the Inopos district.

**The House of the Herm** ④, one of the largest and most luxurious dwellings on Delos, has three storeys along the side of the theatre hill (38). The main entrance is on the north side, to the right of which were found, at the time of excavation, a few remains of an altar and paintings of the *Compitalia*; a masonry altar and a niche against the house opposite probably belonged to the same complex. Off the vestibule were latrines, a small kitchen and a bathroom with a terracotta hip bath. Then comes the courtyard (39), bounded on three sides by Doric porticoes with an upper storey, and on the fourth, a retaining wall with two niches: the larger, where a spring flowed feeding a cistern, housed the statue of a nymph. Opening onto the courtyard, to the north, was a large reception room (*oecus*), that itself gave onto two service rooms and, to the east, a small dining room where couches for banquets were arranged along the walls, on a slightly raised floor. This is the only example to be found on Delos of the *andron* typical of Greek houses of Olynthus and Priene, where the master of the house received his friends for dinner. Notice that the walls of the ground floor were covered with highly elaborate stuccoed and painted decoration and the house was decorated with many divine statues and statuettes including one signed by Praxiteles. Two staircases led to the first floor, where several rooms that have now disappeared opened onto the upper gallery of the three porticoes. Then one could go by a narrower stairway to the second floor made up of rooms of more modest dimensions and decor. In the south-east corner of the first room on the left, a niche sheltered a remarkable herm* with an archaic-style head (now exhibited in the museum, 40). On its inscribed base, the Greek dedication of Dionysios Paconius the Younger slave of Cnaeus is addressed to Hermes and to 'his companions', probably other slaves of the *gens* in a domestic cult college: indeed the text is dated by the mention of 'priest of Artemis Soteira', one Antiochos Paconius. While the exact nature of the group escapes us, the inscription is enlightening on several points: the Italian family of the Paconii lived in the house, the second floor of which was probably the slave quarters; one of them had a high quality statue of Hermes placed there, inspired by archaic models, which says a great deal about his cultural and financial standing despite his servile status; lastly, the slaves were associated with the domestic cults of the Paconii, who seem to have

The Italians on Delos

been particularly fond of the god of commerce. Five other statues or statuettes of Hermes were unearthed in different parts of the building. After observing the final staircase leading to the top door and to the now vanished third floor of the house, we go back down into the courtyard where another herm is raised beneath the western portico (a third pillar, with a juvenile and beardless head, is exhibited in the museum).

The Paconii were a prominent Italian family. We know of twenty-three of its members, six of whom were *magistri* and five contributed to subscriptions for Egyptian gods. Four others were buried on Rheneia and Titus Paconius, the author of the curse tablet mentioned earlier, was one of the family (p. 18 and box 4). While their business is unknown, their home is fine evidence of the private lives of wealthy Italians.

*Leaving the House of the Herm, we turn right and then almost immediately left on the path to the museum. By taking the right fork, we can make a detour by the Sarapieion A and the Terrace of the foreign gods (⟨19⟩, ⟨18⟩, ⟨17⟩) and visit the sanctuaries of the Egyptian and Syrian divinities, which counted many Italians among their faithful (pp. 11–12). From there, we can head for the museum ⟨5⟩ to discover the altars and religious paintings of the* Compitalia, *exhibited in the first room on the left* (**41**).

While rare inscriptions have made it possible to identify some Italian dwellings, quite exceptional **religious paintings** provide a living and colourful picture of their inhabitants: painted on house façades, in niches and on masonry altars set against them, they depict the Roman festival of the *Compitalia*. They were regularly renewed and up to twelve layers can be counted often taking up the same themes. Excavations have brought to light more than thirty sets of paintings in the various districts of Delos almost all of which have now vanished because they are so fragile. There remain drawings, watercolours and photographs as well as a few of the originals exhibited in the museum.

In the Roman world, the *Compitalia* were celebrated at the beginning of January in honour of the Lares Compitales (p. 17). It was a holiday, an occasion for family festivities during which slaves were for once centre stage: they took part in the sacrifice of a pig and a banquet followed. Games, the *ludi compitalicii*, were organized in the streets, bringing together all the neighbourhood. On Delos, this festival was celebrated by the Italians in the family setting, on altars

The Italians on Delos

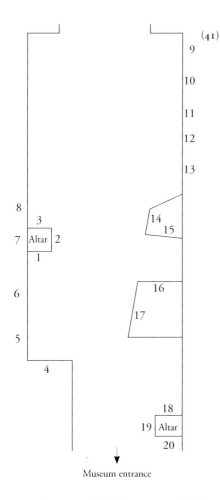

(41)

set up at the doors of houses, but also in the official setting of the association of the *Italici*: although no source confirms it, it is likely that the Competaliasts made a sacrifice in the shrine of the Lares and organized *ludi* on the esplanade of the Agora of the Competaliasts (p. 35). It also seems the cult might have won over devotees of other nationalities or have been influenced by foreign rituals: in some paintings, Greek gods mix with Italian gods and characters sacrifice wearing wreaths in Greek style rather than covering their heads with a fold of their toga as the Romans did. This is why the presence of religious paintings is not a sure sign of an Italian house.

The specimens in the museum give a good idea of how the paintings were laid out and of the main themes portrayed (41). Against the west wall stands a quadrangular altar with the three visible faces painted. The middle face (no. 2) displays, as with all altars, a sacrificial scene, that is poorly preserved but similar to that at the House of the Tulli (37 and 42). In it can be recognized, from left to right, a player of a double *aulos* (a sort of oboe), a small character leading a pig, an altar with a vaulted awning, and three Italians, their heads covered with a fold of their toga, preparing to sacrifice the animal. A slightly different version features on the altar against the eastern wall (no. 19): the figure leading the pig carries a tray with three pieces of fruit on it to the altar.

On the side faces of the altars *ludi compitalicii* are depicted. These were sporting contests: in general wrestlers are shown, as on the east altar (nos 18 and 20)

The haunts of the Italians: from neighbourhood shrines to ostentatious monuments

(42)

(43)

ΚΛΛΜΟϒΓL

(44)

or boxers as on panel no. 10 (**44**). On the right face of the west altar (no. 3), exceptionally, we see a fight between two men armed with spears and shields, evoking gladiators although they are bare headed. The prizes for the victors were hams, amphorae or palms, often laid out beside the fighters: notice the huge amphora to the left of the boxer on panel no. 6 (see also **37**, an amphora and a ham in the foreground).

Against the eastern wall of the room, the entrance to a house on the hill north of the port has been reconstructed ⑪: to the left of the door, a niche housed offerings or served for lighting and on the right were two altars (not reproduced here). On either side, the owners had commissioned a total of nine sets of paintings that were removed layer by layer and fixed on the panels exhibited on the walls (nos 5–17). They repeat, with a few variations, the themes common to all pictures: accordingly the Lares Compitales (nos 7 and 8, see p. 17 and **12**), dancing with a rhyton in their hand, are painted above the altar because the sacrifice was intended for them. Two other gods are present: Mercury, the protector of the entrance, is shown to the right of the door walking and holding a purse (no. 5, fragmentary) and Heracles, who seems often to preside over the *ludi*, appears in four successive layers (nos 13, 12, 11, 10, see **44**) with his club and lionskin. But the most recent paintings in the set exhibit several original features suggesting the cult might have been taken up by a new owner of the premises, less familiar with Italian traditions. The scene of the sacrifice (no. 16) is not found on the altar but on the wall, the figures are not veiled but wreathed, as in the Greek rite, and a trumpet player has replaced the double *aulos* player (**45**). Where the earlier layers showed Heracles and scenes of combat, we now see a rider on a galloping horse, followed by a runner holding the animal's tail (no. 15): it may be an equestrian event (**46**). Lastly, the other two panels show a man climbing a palm tree (no. 14) and a small figure taking fruit from a glass bowl on a table (no. 17, see **43**).

Numerous graffiti and a few painted inscriptions can be seen on the various layers. Above the three wreathed figures (no. 16) are the first letters of their Greek names or nicknames (Theog[enes?], Hip[pias?], Iason), indicative of Italian slaves or freedmen or of Greeks having adopted an Italian cult (**45**). Lastly, at the bottom right of layers nos 10 and 11 (**44**), a burlesque figure with a big belly designated by his name 'Kalamodryas' is probably to be identified with a famous athlete of the early first century BC.

The haunts of the Italians: from neighbourhood shrines to ostentatious monuments

*After viewing pictures of the* Compitalia, *in the next room can be seen the busts of the House of the Seals* (p. 26 and **21**) *and the beardless herm of the House of the Herm* (p. 44); *in the third room the statue of Ofellius* (p. 14 and **10**) *is displayed and in the fourth, the archaic herm of the House of the Herm* (p. 42 and **40**). *On the right, on leaving the museum, it is possible to make quite a long detour via the Stadium district. At the end of the path to the east, we can visit the gymnasium* (14), *frequented by the Italians* (pp. 10–11 and **7**), *before arriving at the house of the Tullii* (15) (p. 40).

*On arriving back at the north-west corner of the museum esplanade, we can go along East Street on the left to see the monument in honour of C. Billienus* (7) (p. 18 and **13**) *and visit the House of Spurius Stertinius* (6) (p. 40 and **36**), *the vestibule of which is behind the second column of the portico bordering the houses, on the left side of the street. From there we visit the Agora of the Italians going in by the eastern entrance* (8).

## THE 'AGORA OF THE ITALIANS', A PLACE FOR GATHERING AND OSTENTATION

Archaeologists have mistakenly named 'agora' the huge building erected by the Italians at a disputed date – around 130 for some and a little before 100 BC

(47)

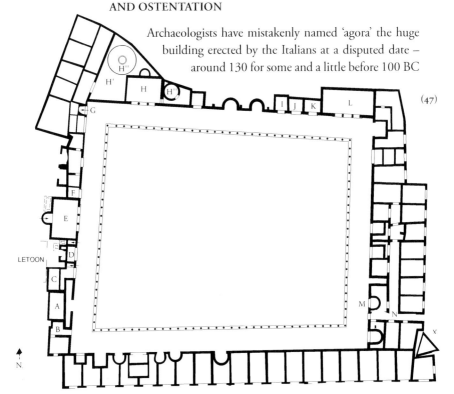

for others – and that was probably never completed (pp. 2–3 and 47). If a mutilated inscription is to be believed, the Ancients called it rather *Italike pastas*, 'the Italian portico' and the vagueness of the name reflects its absence of architectural specificity. That is why the function of the Agora of the Italians has been and still is the subject of much debate. It has been seen as a meeting place or a palaestra reserved for the Italians alone, a slave market or a leisure garden open to all, or again a multifunctional building serving for leisure, commerce and for the temporary housing of merchants and their wares, whether Italian or affiliated.

What is certain is that the construction was a long drawn out affair, led by and for the association of the *Italici*. Once the huge trapezoidal central courtyard had been delimited, on land that was probably reclaimed by backfilling the lake, in the very centre of the city – fresh evidence of the favour the Italian community enjoyed among the Athenians – the construction of the storeyed porticoes (48) was divided among eight groups of generous donors whose names are inscribed on the entablature blocks, followed by the dedication 'to Apollo and to the *Italici*'.

On the ground floor, porticoes of marble Doric columns can be seen on the four sides of the courtyard: the north portico with its distinctive stylobate of red lava-rock on the north side was financed by the banker Philostratos of Ascalon (pp. 12–13) and the one on the west by Caius Ofellius (p. 14). All four were topped by galleries with Ionic pillars, that were walled up and probably had windows: they were presented by four groups of donors, including two colleges of *magistri*. Many of the upper pillars and their capitals can be seen set aside in the south portico; the inscribed entablature blocks of the ground and upper floors are aligned in the other porticoes.

Beneath the porticoes various *exedrae* and niches open up: their construction, furnishing and decoration were also entrusted to various individuals in several stages, although the chronology is not known in full. The whole looks

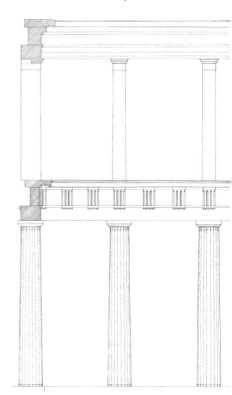

very scrappy: an *exedra* is placed in the centre of the western portico and two others below the northern portico, with no symmetry at all; niches of varied dimensions, rectangular and semi-circular, were set out here and there between long stretches of solid wall; those of the south portico were built encroaching on the shops that backed onto the Agora of the Italians on the southern street. Many attempts have been made to reconstruct the initial design but the irregularities of the ground plan of the building can be explained by the piecemeal financing. It must have been built step by step to meet the proposals of each contributor and try to satisfy their requirements in terms of placing, shape and size.

*Exedrae* E, H and L whose wide bays were divided by two columns between Ionic doorposts are furnished with marble benches, some engraved with their donors' names. They may have been merely for passers-by, or for business meetings or conferences. The *exedra* of the north-east (L) was built by Philostratos of Ascalon and probably housed the statue the *Italici* had erected to him (p. 13). That of the north-west (H) served as a vestibule to the *thermae* (see 52), whose presence indicates the building was a place of leisure for the resident Italians or a place of sojourn for traders passing through. On the right and left of the vestibule were rooms for sweating, bathing or relaxing: the smaller of the two circular rooms

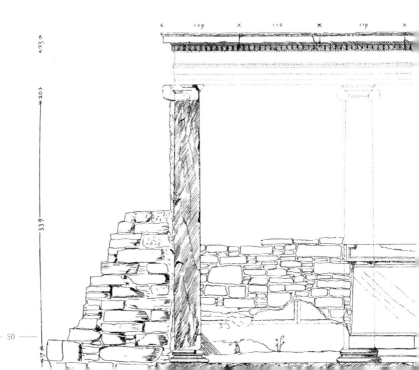

with terracotta tiling (H") was probably the *laconicum*, a dry room financed by two former Hermaists (p. 27 and 22). Lastly, the western *exedra* (E, **49**) housed in its central niche the statue of the Roman proconsul C. Cluvius.

The many richly decorated niches were meant for statues of personalities honoured by the *Italici* or by individuals. Several still have their inscribed bases. Mention can be made especially of the base for the marble likeness of Caius Ofellius (F, p. 14 and **10**), with the dedication of the Italians (on the crowning) and the signature of the two Athenian sculptors, Dionysios, son of Timarchides, and Timarchides, son of Polycletes (on the base itself). The statue was embedded in the marble basin still visible on the upper face. Another statue, discovered in niche J and now exhibited in the National Museum of Athens, is of a fighting Gaul (**50**), attesting to the taste of the Italians of Delos for the art of Pergamon further to Attalus III's bequest of his kingdom to Rome.

Certain niches, reconstructed after the excavation, are adorned with mosaics of varying quality. In niche K, the flooring shows a bronze hydria* set on a base, a palm and other unidentified items, framed by bands of meanders and braids forming a carpet. The donor's name, Publius Satricanius, son of Publius, is written in Greek with black tesserae on the white ground of the central

panel (51). Similarly we can read the name of Lucius Orbius, son of Marcus, of the Roman tribe Horatia, on the mosaic in niche D.

The central courtyard was not paved and archaeological soundings and geophysical surveys have not revealed any remains. Was it a garden planted with trees? There is no sign of this. An inscription engraved on the doorpost of the vestibule of the *thermae* (H, 52) suggests that the immense space of packed earth could have had another use: this fragmentary Latin dedication comes from a college of twelve *magistri* (Hermaists, Apolloniasts and Poseidoniasts) commemorating the construction of a part of the building and the celebration, at their expense, of *ludi*. These were obviously not the *ludi compitalicii* organized by the Competaliasts, the college of slaves and freedmen, of whom no trace is found in the Agora of the Italians. The *ludi*, in Rome, were public games, theatrical shows, sporting competitions or chariot races, organized in the context of religious festivals or laid on for the people by magistrates. The immense courtyard of the Agora of the Italians may have been the venue for events financed by the *magistri* of Mercury, Apollo and Neptune, without it being possible to determine the nature of these *ludi*. It is not impossible either that gladiatorial fights (*munera*) were held: a plaque found elsewhere on Delos bears the incised drawing of a gladiator and an inscription recalling the victories of one Marcus Caecilius Epagathos.

The Agora of the Italians had three entrances: two vestibules, at the south-west and south-east corners (B and N) and a propylaeum (A), a monumental entrance with four Doric columns that was added subsequently and whose articulation with the building remains a puzzle. Outside, along the street are a score of shops that back on to the southern portico: although no text specifies what they were for, it is likely they were rented out by the *Italici* to tradesmen or craftsmen so as to bring in a regular income for the association.

At the end of this journey through the haunts of the Italians, it is worth underscoring the emblematic character of the Agora of the Italians. Whatever its purposes may have been – and all the evidence is that they were plentiful and combined leisure, business and hospitality –, it was above all a symbol of the power of

ΠΛΙΟΣ                 ΠΟΠΛΙΟΥ
ΚΑΝΙΟΣ              ΥΙΟΣ

the *Italici* on Delos. By sharing among its members the construction of the porticoes, *exedrae* and *thermae*, by allowing them to erect statues of eminent figures in a sumptuous setting, by displaying their names everywhere in stone, the association of the *Italici* provided them with a showcase where they could display their success, wealth and influence. It is obvious, under the circumstances, that the Agora of the Italians was open to all: what interest would the Italians have had in reserving such ostentation for themselves? The precinct was not a closed associative building like the Clubhouse of the Poseidoniasts of Berytos, which is why no administrative documents or shrines were to be found there: the association's headquarters is to be sought elsewhere. It was simply a huge showcase where Athenians and foreigners living on the island, as well as visiting Athenian and Roman magistrates, were received with pomp and which, in a cramped city with a teeming population and ubiquitous trading, could certainly cater for multiple needs.

*On the way back to the mole, we might stop on the Agora of Theophrastos* (9) *to see the base of the statue of Theophrastos (p. 18 and* **14***), the* Poseideion *and its altar* (10) *(p. 17) and the base of the statue of Heracles dedicated by the Hermaists, Apolloniasts and Poseidoniasts (***11*** and* box 3*). It is also possible to make a detour to visit the Clubhouse of the Poseidoniasts of Berytos* (12) *(pp. 13–14 and* **9***).*

# *Conclusion*

However prosperous they may have been, the Italians of Delos were subject to the fluctuations of economic networks and it seems that, from the early first century BC, Delos began to lose out to the Italian port of Puteoli in trade between the Orient and Italy. But the island fell victim above all to two successive catastrophes that are well attested by literary and archaeological sources. In the war that opposed Rome to the king of Pontus Mithridates Eupator, Delos broke from Athens and refused, under the influence of the Italians, to side with Mithridates: in the autumn of 88 BC, he took and plundered Delos, killed 20,000 men, mostly Italians according to Appian, and carried off the women and children into slavery. Twenty years later, in 69 BC, the soldiery of the pirate Athenodoros, in the pay of Mithridates, sacked the island again: in response, the Roman legate Caius Triarius had a rampart built encircling a part of the city.

Although their scale has plainly been exaggerated by ancient historians, many marks remain of these two catastrophes. In 88, the Italian buildings were subject

to much deliberate damage: the statue of the Roman magistrate C. Billienus (**13**) was mutilated, as were many honorific monuments of the Agora of the Italians that still bear the signature 'Aristandros of Paros repaired it'. It may have been at this time that the relief of the altar of the Lares (**29**) was hammered on the Agora of the Competaliasts. As for the House of the Seals (p. 26), it was probably burnt in 69 after the two busts of its owners had been damaged (**21**); it was never rebuilt, suggesting its occupants left the island or perished there.

The continuation of this story is poorly known: eager to repair the damage and restart their business, the Italians received the visit and aid of the proconsul Sulla shortly after the catastrophe of 88; but they largely abandoned the island after 69, because the profit they found there was no longer equal to the investment needed for a second recovery. Pompey's victory against the pirates in 67 and the creation of Roman provinces in the regions that furnished slaves (especially Syria in 64) meant the sources of supply for the Delian market ran dry. Traces of Italian presence can still be found until the middle of the first century BC, with in particular an inscription of the Hermaists recalling the dedication of a temple and statues to Hermes in 57/6. But the rare honorific monuments preserved were by then dedicated by the Athenians and other inhabitants of the island, without any specific mention of the Italians. Where then had the plethoric *gentes* of the Paconii, Tullii or Aemilii gone? While some, as natives of the peninsula's wealthy commercial cities, probably returned to their homeland, others left to develop their activities in busier Aegean ports: from the end of the first century, we find the *nomina gentilicia* of the Italians of Delos in Macedonia, the Peloponnese and Asia Minor. Delos remained throughout Roman times a famed place of pilgrimage under the control of Athens but the prosperity of the cosmopolitan port that had so attracted the Italians was but a distant memory.

The Italians on Delos

# *Glossary*

**Agora**: public square where retail trade was conducted under the supervision of magistrates called agoranomes.

**Architrave**: an entablature block in a temple or portico resting directly on columns.

***Bucranium*, plur. *bucrania***: carved ox head decorating altars or architectural friezes.

**Campanian peristyle**: porticoes surrounding a courtyard characterized by the columns (or pillars) being raised on low walls.

**Cenotaph**: empty funeral monument commemorating a deceased person whose body has not been found.

**College** (Latin *collegium*): group of persons taking on a same official function collectively. In the Roman world, political and administrative responsibilities were often collegial.

**Consuls**: supreme magistrates of the Roman state, exercising civil and military power. Elected for one year, the two consuls gave their name to the year.

**Crepis**: two or three steps leading up to a temple, portico, etc.

**Curse tablet**: copper or lead plate on which a curse or spell was carved before it was thrown into a well or tomb for the gods of the underworld.

**Dedication**: inscription engraved on an offering and indicating the name of the donor, any function, the addressee, the nature of the offering, the date, etc. **Votive** (or religious) **dedications** were addressed to divinities whereas **honorific dedications** paid tribute to an individual, a statue of whom was generally erected.

**Dioscuri**: name given to the twin gods Castor and Pollux, protectors of seafarers.

***Emporion***: area of the port for wholesale (international) commerce under the supervision of a magistrate known as the *epimeletes* of the *emporion*.

**Entablature**: in a temple or portico, the blocks between the columns and the roof (or the upper portico).

***Ephebeia***: physical and intellectual education given by the city to young men aged 18 to 20 (**ephebes**) in the gymnasium.

***Epimeletes* of the island**: as from 167 BC, the principal Athenian magistrate on Delos tasked with executing decisions of the assembly, religious and financial matters, etc. Elected for one year, he was eponymous, that is, the indication of his name in the inscriptions served as a date marker.

**Epitaph**: inscription engraved on a funerary monument.

**Ethnic**: adjective added to a person's name and indicating their city of origin.

***Euergetes***: benefactor putting their fortune at the service of a community (city, association, etc.) and honoured for their acts of civic patronage (**euergetism**: financing of monuments, festivals, etc.).

***Exedra***: room opening via a wide bay beneath a portico; often furnished with marble benches, it served as a place for meeting, teaching or relaxing.

**Freedman**: former slave freed by his master, now his 'patron' towards whom he retains certain duties.

**Gens, plur. gentes**: in the Roman world, family, lineage whose members bore the same *nomen gentilicium*.

**Herm**: monument sculpted in the shape of a pillar topped by a bust of Hermes and with a male member on the front face: erected in the street, on the agora or sometimes in a private building, it was of a sacred character and protected the premises.

**Hydria**: a three-handled jug for carrying water.

**Inscription**: text engraved in a durable material, usually stone, sometimes metal. Delian inscriptions were usually written in ancient Greek or sometimes in Latin.

**Koinon**: Greek word designating an association.

**Laconicum**: in Roman baths, a circular room where people would transpire in a hot dry atmosphere.

**Libation**: rite consisting in the offering of a drink to a divinity, by pouring on the altar a mix of wine, milk, oil or honey.

**Ludi**: in the Roman world, public games organized as part of religious festivals or entertainment sponsored by magistrates for the people.

**Magister, plur. magistri, magistres or magistreis**: title given in the Roman world to representatives of associations who held their office collegially. On Delos, the *magistri* of Mercury were called Hermaists in Greek, those of Neptune, Poseidoniasts, those of Apollo, Apolloniasts and those of the Lares Compitales, Competaliasts.

**Monopteros**: circular edifice with an open colonnade (without a central room) generally housing a statue.

**Naiskos**: small temple.

**Naukleros, plur. naukleroi**: owner of a merchant vessel.

**Niche**: in a portico, small room inaccessible to the public and housing a statue.

**Nomen gentilicium**: family name common to all members of a *gens*.

**Offering**: object or monument dedicated to a divinity.

**Pastophorion**: in Egyptian shrines, room for the priests and possibly the faithful.

**Peculium**: amount of money put aside by a slave to buy their freedom from their master.

**Proconsul**: former consul, governor of a Roman province.

**Prostyle**: (temple) with columns on the façade only, raised ahead of the wall ends (antae).

**Rhyton**: vase in the shape of a horn, used for drinking wine or making libations*.

**Sanctuary**: sacred space, delimited by a wall or boundary stones, dedicated to the cult of a divinity.

**Seal**: stamp on which are engraved an image and sometimes a name. Signatories of a contract on papyrus placed their seal on a piece of unbaked clay to guarantee its authenticity. When the House of the Seals on Delos was set on fire, the papyri were burnt and the clay tags baked, preserving them.

**Sekoma**: stone counter for measuring out oil, wine or grain for sale.

**Shrine**: small cult edifice or room for worship within a building serving some other main purpose.

**Subscription**: form of financing by involving a large number of people in the construction of an edifice or other costly undertaking; the **list of subscribers** and the amounts paid were engraved on a stele to commemorate their generosity.

# Further reading

P. Bruneau et al. (eds.), *Délos : île sacrée et ville cosmopolite* (1996).

P. Bruneau, J. Ducat, *Guide de Délos*, 4th ed. (2005).

M.-T. Couilloud, *Les monuments funéraires de Rhénée, EAD* XXX (1974).

J. Delorme, 'La Maison dite de l'Hermès, à Délos : étude architecturale', *BCH* 77 (1953), pp. 444–496.

P. Ernst, *Recherches sur les pratiques culturelles des Italiens à Délos aux II^e et I^er siècles a.C.* (2019).

A. Erskine, *A Companion to the Hellenistic World* (2007).

C. Habicht, *Athens from Alexander to Antony*, chap. 10 'Athenian Delos' (1999).

C. Hasenohr, 'Les *Compitalia* à Délos', *BCH* 127.1 (2003), pp. 167–249.

C. Hasenohr, 'The Italian Associations at Delos: Religion, Trade, Politics and Social Cohesion (2nd–1st c. BC)', in A. Cazemiers, S. Stalka (eds.), *Associations and Religion in Context: The Hellenistic and Roman Eastern Mediterranean* (2021), pp. 77–89.

P. Karvonis, 'Les installations commerciales dans la ville de Délos à l'époque hellénistique', *BCH* 132.1 (2008), pp. 153–219.

C. Le Roy, 'Encore l'Agora des Italiens à Délos', in M.-M. Mactoux, É. Gény (eds.), *Mélanges Pierre Lévêque* 7 (1993), pp. 183–208.

J. Marcadé (ed.), *Sculptures déliennes* (1996).

C. Müller, C. Hasenohr (eds.), *Les Italiens dans le monde grec* (2002).

M. Trümper, 'Where the Non-Delians met in Delos: The Meeting-Places of Foreign Associations and Ethnic Communities in Late Hellenistic Delos', in O. van Nijf, R. Alston (eds.), *Political Culture in the Greek City after the Classical Age* (2011), pp. 49–100.

M. Zarmakoupi, 'Hellenistic & Roman Delos: The City & Its Emporion', *Archaeological Reports* 61 (2015), pp. 115–132.

# Cited texts

The Italians on Delos

# List of illustrations

**Map 1** — The haunts of the Italians (after J.-C. Moretti [ed.], *Atlas*, 2015, pl. 5).

**Map 2** — The haunts of the Italians: walking tour route (after J.-C. Moretti [ed.], *Atlas*, 2015, pl. 7).

**pp. 2–3** — View of the Agora of the Italians, with the Lion Terrace in the foreground and Mount Kynthos in the background (photo 1910).

1. Aerial view of the port, sanctuary of Apollo and housing districts (photo J.-C. Moretti, C. Gaston).
2. Some home cities of the Italians of Delos (after *EAD* XXX, fig. 28).
3. Funerary stele of Timocrates Raecius, slave of Nemerius.
4. Base of statue of Quintus Tullius on a cylindrical base in house IC of the Stadium district (photo C. Hasenohr).
5. Funerary stele of Tertia Horaria (Mykonos Archaeological Museum, photo C. Hasenohr).
6. Funerary stele of Furia (photo P. Collet).
7. Delos gymnasium (photo C. Hasenohr).
8. Relief of Artemis Soteira dedicated by Spurius Stertinius (photo P. Collet).
9. Plan of the Clubhouse of the Poseidoniasts of Berytos (*Guide de Délos*, p. 229, fig. 63).
10. Statue of Caius Ofellius Ferus (photo P. Collet).
11. Base of statue of Hercules (Heracles) dedicated by the Hermaists, Apolloniasts and Poseidoniasts (photo. C. Hasenohr).
12. The Lares Compitales: painting on the façade of the house opposite the House of the Hill (Delos Museum, photo C. Hasenohr).
13. Statue of Caius Billienus (photo C. Hasenohr).
14. Monument in honour of the *epimeletes* Theophrastos (photo C. Hasenohr).
15. Delian graffiti showing merchant vessels (L. Basch, *Le musée imaginaire de la marine antique*, Institut hellénique pour la préservation de la tradition nautique, 1987, pp. 374–380).
16. Funerary stele of Spurius Granius (*EAD* XXX, pl. 67).
17. *Sekoma* of C. Julius Caesar (photo C. Hasenohr).
18. Italian amphorae discovered on Delos: **a.** Brindisian amphora (oil), **b.** Dressel 1A amphora (wine), **c.** Dressel 1C amphora (wine), **d.** Lamboglia 2 amphora (wine). Drawings N. Sigalas.
19. Aerial view of the Agora of the Delians (photo J.-C. Moretti, C. Gaston).
20. Delian seals bearing Roman names (M.-F. Boussac, 'Sceaux déliens', *Revue archéologique*, 1988, p. 324).
21. Busts of two Italians (?) discovered in the House of the Seals (photo P. Collet).
22. Dedication of the *laconicum* in the *thermae* of the Agora of the Italians.
23. Plan of the Agora of the Competaliasts (after J.-C. Moretti [ed.], *Atlas*, 2015, pl. 25).
24. The Ionic naiskos of the Hermaists (photo C. Hasenohr).
25. Reconstruction of the Ionic naiskos of the Hermaists (drawing G. Poulsen).

26. The offertory box of the Ionic naiskos (J. Hatzfeld, 'Les Italiens résidant à Délos', *BCH* 36, 1912, p. 201).
27. The monopteros of the Competaliasts and its peribolos (photo C. Hasenohr).
28. Reconstruction of the monopteros of the Competaliasts and its peribolos (3D modelling and credits: F. F. Müller, F. Comte, Ausonius UMR 5607 - Labex LaScArBx ANR-10-Labex-52).
29. The altar of the Lares Compitales (photo C. Hasenohr).
30. Entablature of the Doric naiskos of the Hermaists (photo C. Hasenohr).
31. Reconstructed elevation of the upper part of the Doric naiskos of the Hermaists (drawing B. Sagnier).
32. The altar of Hercules (Heracles) (photo C. Hasenohr).
33. Reconstruction of the Agora of the Competaliasts viewed from the south (3D modelling F. Comte, Ausonius UMR 5607 - Labex LaScArBx ANR-10- Labex-52).
34. Plan of the seafront warehouses (after J.-C. Moretti [ed.], *Atlas*, 2015, pl. 27).
35. Warehouse γ (photo C. Hasenohr).
36. Niche in the house of Spurius Stertinius (photo C. Hasenohr).
37. Altar, bench and Italian religious paintings at the entrance to house IC in the Stadium district in 1912 (photo C. Avezou).
38. The House of the Herm (photo C. Hasenohr).
39. Reconstruction of the courtyard of the House of the Herm (drawing Y. Fomine).
40. Archaic-style head of Hermes of the House of the Herm (photo P. Collet).
41. Locations of the Italian religious paintings in the museum.
42. Sacrificial scene painted on the outside altar of house IC of the Stadium district (water colour M. Bulard).
43. Character taking fruit from a glass bowl (layer no. 17, photo C. Hasenohr).
44. Heracles presiding over a boxing contest at the *ludi compitalicii* (layer no. 10, photo C. Hasenohr).
45. Sacrificial scene and trumpet player (layer no. 16, photo C. Hasenohr).
46. Equestrian event? (layer no. 15, photo C. Hasenohr).
47. Reconstructed plan of the Agora of the Italians (*Guide de Délos*, p. 222, fig. 60).
48. Reconstruction of the porticoes of the Agora of the Italians (*Guide de Délos*, p. 222, fig. 60).
49. Elevation drawing of the west *exedra* (E) of the Agora of the Italians (E. Lapalus, *EAD* XIX, 1939, fig. 37).
50. Statue of the fighting Gaul of the Agora of the Italians. Athens National Archaeological Museum (photo P. Collet).
51. The mosaic of Publius Satricanius (water colour M. Bulard).
52. The courtyard of the Agora of the Italians, seen from the vestibule of the *thermae* (photo J.-C. Moretti).
53. The Agora of the Competaliasts from the east (photo C. Hasenohr).

Iconographic credits: EFA, unless otherwise stated.

# Contents

Printed in September 2021
by n.v. PEETERS s.a.
ISBN: 978-2-86958-551-5
Legal deposit: 4th quarter 2021

Front cover: religious painting from the 'Warehouse with the bath': Lare and boxing match of the *ludi compitalicii* (water colour by G. Simões Da Fonseca, after M. Bulard, *Peintures murales et mosaïques de Délos* [1908], pl. IV).

Director: Véronique Chankowski – Publishing manager: Bertrand Grandsagne – Editorial follow up: EFA, Pauline Gibert-Massoni then Iris Granet-Cornée – Graphic design, prepress: EFA, Guillaume Fuchs – Translation and editing of texts in english: Christopher Sutcliffe